Big Ideas for Small Sunday Schools

BIG
IDEAS FOR
SMALL
SUNDAY SCHOOLS

by

Ralph L. McIntyre

BAKER BOOK HOUSE
Grand Rapids, Michigan

Contents

Preface

In March of 1962, while I was teaching school in Montana, my wife and I felt the call of the Lord to move to Buffalo, Wyo., and labor in a small church there. I applied for a teaching position at the local high school, was accepted, and that fall we moved to Buffalo.

Soon both my wife and I were teaching Sunday school classes and I had been elected Sunday school superintendent. Our total average attendance at that time was about 50. That average didn't vary much for several years; we remained a typical "small" Sunday school, trying to "hold our own."

In 1968, through the efforts of a number of people who were interested in seeing our school grow, we began to see things happen. Since that time our average attendance has increased some 350 percent to a current average of 175. This increase has come about through many factors, and this book is an attempt to tell you about some of them.

In attempting to locate new ideas to help get our Sunday school going, we read a variety of materials from pamphlets to books. During this study process we noticed that the majority of the materials on the market were aimed at the very large Sunday school in the metropolitan areas. We have tried to adapt some of these ideas to our own situation. Other ideas presented here are original with us, while still others have been gleaned from various meetings and conversations. Most of these ideas have been highly successful; a few have been miserable failures. Some of the "failures" have been included, because we feel that they would be successful if used with the proper approach. We have also come to realize that not all ideas work in every situation; but if a Sunday school tries enough new ideas, success will outshine failure.

It is my earnest desire as superintendent of a "small" (less than 200 average attendance) Sunday school, in a "small" (population 3,500) town, to share these ideas with others. Our prayer is that these ideas will help many "small" Sunday schools like ours to find new life, and that this new life will enable them to move forward numerically, financially, and spiritually.

Many of the ideas included here, I previously prepared for use in various publications of the Wesleyan church. I am grateful for the permission granted to reuse them in this more permanent form.

—R. L. M.

Chapter 1

Why Sunday School?

The only people who think that Sunday school is dead or dying are those people who *are* dead or dying, spiritually. Until we all know and practice everything that there is to learn from the Bible, we will *need* Sunday schools. Your Sunday school is at its present size because you desire it to be that size. God's Word declares that He will grant us our hearts' desire. Do you desire a growing Sunday school? He has it for you! God wants your school to grow. We know that He wants us to share Him with others, and what better way to teach people about Him than through the Sunday school? God will help your Sunday school to grow numerically and spiritually if you will let Him.

For too long we have listened to the devil's lie, that somehow spirituality goes hand in hand with smallness. There is *no* spiritual blessing in being small! God wants us to prosper in His work. Ps. 1:3 tells us that whatever the godly man does shall prosper, and we are advised in 3 John 2 that above all things it is hoped that we will prosper. Mark 11:24 states that whatever we desire when we pray, if we believe, we shall have our desire. Do you desire to see your Sunday school grow? Pray! Believe! Work! Concentrate on success! Don't accept mediocrity and failure! Growth can be yours!

We must develop the attitude that this is the best day of our lives. Yesterday is gone. Tomorrow has not arrived, so this is the best day. "This is the day which the Lord hath made; we will rejoice and be glad in it." If we believe this, people will want what we have.

Concentrate on succeeding rather than failing. The reason a lot of people are failing is that they are working at it. One of the foremost problems that one must face in a small Sunday school is a lack of interest. This may have developed from years of a steady or declining average attendance. For so long we have been content to just replace those who pass on or move away. When this lack of interest infects the laity, it is serious; if it also occurs in the ministry of your church, it is disastrous!

In developing any of the methods described in this book, it is important that you, your staff, and your pastor be enthused about the project and its expected result. Presenting the pyramid shown on the next page will help illustrate to your pastor and personnel what an increase in Sunday school can mean to every avenue of your church. (You might tell *your* pastor that in *our* case the pastor's salary has quadrupled since we began stressing Sunday school!)

When the base is broadened, all other areas will soon show an increase. Shorten the base and all other areas will soon feel the effects. It works—we've tried it!

When we first began our Sunday school enrollment drive, we announced a special staff meeting for a date some weeks distant, and urged all our staff to be present. At this meeting we presented the pyramid and the obvious need for increased Sunday school attendance. We had also con-

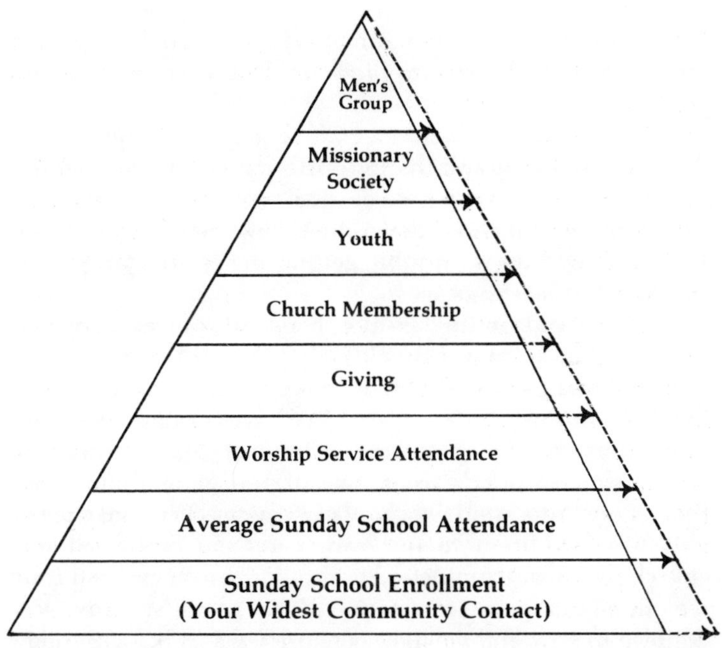

structed a large graph showing our average Sunday school attendance for the previous 10 years. Except for a few ups and downs, it was essentially a straight line. In addition, we had constructed a small class graph for each teacher, showing the average attendance in his or her class for the previous year.

After much discussion and a season of prayer, we asked each teacher to write on a slip of paper the number by which he thought he could increase his average attendance in the next six months. At that time we had nine classes. We asked each teacher to be very realistic, to write only the number that he could *really* believe the Lord for. After the slips were collected and totaled, the count was 20—about 2 per class. This wouldn't be a large number for a big Sunday school, but for our small group it represented a projected increase of 30 percent in a six-month period! Certainly it was a greater projected growth than we had ever experienced previously.

Each month we met as a staff to graph individual class averages, and to graph the total attendance. We praised the Lord for those classes where the goal was being met, and had special prayer for those that were falling short. Interest was high, and we had no trouble getting the entire staff out to our monthly meetings.

At the end of the six-month period, our average had climbed to 89 from our previous 60, an increase of 29! This represented a gain of almost 50 percent! From that point on, faith and enthusiasm were ours! We have continued to grow since that time to our current average of 175. During this period we also purchased a new parsonage and converted the old one into Sunday school classrooms. We constructed a 100-seat addition to our sanctuary and renovated our church basement completely to provide three new, and four remodeled, carpeted classrooms. The pastor's study was doubled in size, and we have constructed a 28' x 72' Sunday school classroom building with a full basement.

We're currently shooting for an average attendance of 500, and when we reach that we'll expand some more. Far-fetched? In our little town of 3,500 people, there are at least 2,000 people who are *not* in a Sunday school or church service of any kind on Sunday morning. We want our share of those 2,000 souls! How many people are unchurched in your town on a typical Sunday morning? They are yours for the taking!

We are sometimes criticized because we stress "counting people." In fact, one dear brother used the old cliché that they were "striving for increased spirituality in his church" that year. I noticed in his quarterly report that his average attendance was down by 20! People are important! That is our basic concern. Sunday school *is* people. The more people, the more the Sunday school will accomplish. If counting people is carnal, why are we told how many people were converted at Pentecost? We count people because people count!

<h3 style="text-align:center">WAYS TO BROADEN THE BASE</h3>

First of all, if you decide to graph your attendance, be sure to break it down by classes. Our first proposed increase of 30 percent didn't look nearly so large when it was figured out at only two per class. What Sunday school teacher couldn't increase his average attendance by two in the next six months? What would it do for your Sunday school if you multiplied your number of classes by two and added that to your average attendance?

On a recent Sunday we had "Top 20 Sunday" (described later in this book). Briefly, each class attempted to have an attendance of 20 on that day. When the dust settled and we finished counting heads, we had an attendance of 262 packed into a building with a capacity of 200. Our Sunday school average at that time was 166.

Second, start your drive at a time of the year when you would normally expect an increase in Sunday school. In our area, this would be from October to December, or March to June. This will almost guarantee an increase and will help you generate enthusiasm among your members.

Third, *never talk negatively!* "Think positive." If you'll just look, you can always find something to praise the Lord for. In talking to people about your Sunday school, never say anything discouraging. Praise the pastor, the superintendent, the Sunday school officers, the teachers, the students, and so forth. Always look up! Things are going great —Sunday school never looked better—things are beginning to move—people are responding—*talk it up!* Be enthusiastic! People want to come where the action is. Talk about how

13

the Lord is going to bless your Sunday school, and watch
Him do just that!

Fourth, contact new families. We in small towns have
an advantage here. In a town of 10,000 or less, your Sunday
school is within easy walking or driving distance of every
family in town. That means that anyone in your town who
doesn't attend Sunday school is a prospect! Our pastor contacts every new family that moves into town. The local
electric company, gas company, water department, Chamber
of Commerce, and so forth, will have a record of every new
family. Our pastor then makes a call on the new family and
invites them to Sunday school and church. Many times that
is the first invitation that they have received since moving
to their new home, and they soon begin attending our Sunday school.

Fifth, contact absentees. Our teachers have agreed to
contact every member of their class who is absent on Sunday morning, before the following Sunday. On Sunday
afternoon our absentee secretary (the Sunday school superintendent and his wife had this job before personnel became
available) makes out an absentee slip in duplicate listing the
name, address, and telephone number of the absentee, and
the teacher's name. One copy goes to the teacher, and the
other copy goes to the pastor. The following Sunday morning the teacher's copy is turned in, along with a notation of
the type of contact made and the reason for the absence.
These are then filed by the pastor. The duplicate copy gives
us a check to be sure that the absentee has been contacted.
These contacts enable the pastor to contact other families in
the community.

We don't expect the pastor to do all the calling. After
all, he is the *shepherd* of the flock, and shepherds don't produce sheep; sheep produce sheep! It's our job, too! In a
recent week, 376 personal invitations were issued by Sunday

school members. For one person, that would represent over 60 per day for 6 days. Many hands make light work!

In our young adult class, a class secretary makes out the absentee slips during class. The duplicate goes to the pastor, while the originals are passed around the class for the class members to voluntarily take. The teacher then assumes the responsibility for the slips that remain. Usually, however, they are all taken before they ever make one trip around the classroom.

Barriers to Sunday School Growth

There are some barriers to Sunday school growth; but if you're aware of them you can avoid them, or tear them down. Lack of unity of purpose, poor planning, misplaced priorities, and faulty objectives will be barriers to avoid.

Many churches are steeped in tradition. Unless a Sunday school is willing to be flexible in her attitudes, current in her planning, uninhibited by her past, willing to pioneer, and is challenged by the needs of the world and her community, she will never make much impact on society. Seven simple words that people use to resist change are *We've never done it that way before.* Attitudes like this will kill progress and must be changed or overcome.

Another barrier to progress in a Sunday school is frequent pastoral change. This is a common problem in small churches. A constant changing of pastors can do nothing but keep a church off-balance, confused, and always in a state of uncertainty. A pastor must have a long pastorate to develop a foundation for a strong, solid growth that continues year after year. A pastor must build a solid support for his ideas, convictions, and program. He must win the respect and confidence of his followers before he can make strides in church building. It is very difficult for churches to adjust to new leadership every two or three years. It weakens a church's fellowship.

Too many pastors try to move away from problems (which is really impossible). Pulpit changing usually means swapping one set of problems for another. In essence, the only problems are people. If one can't find solutions to such problems in one place, he will not likely make it elsewhere.

Of all the barriers that will need to be overcome, negativeness should probably be number one on the list. Sunday school leaders are often afflicted with bad attitudes. They are found whining, complaining, and singing the blues. They sit on top of "Defeat Hill" licking their wounds and blaming everyone everywhere for their defeats. They let the least difficulty throw them. Eighty percent of the workers in churches are right on the verge of quitting all the time. They are looking for an opportunity to get out gracefully.

I challenge you to move out for Jesus! Start planning your strategy to knock down all the barriers that are hindering progress in your leadership and in your church. You must believe victory possible before you will ever be able to lead others in the victory march.

Today is the greatest opportunity that you will ever have. Opportunity never *comes*—it's *here!*

Always remember—you will never teach a greater Sunday school class than the one you teach now. The greatest mission field in the world is where you are serving. If you can't do it there, you probably couldn't do it anywhere.

Chapter 2

Those Special Days

Some writers seem to feel it is not good to have a special emphasis on a normally "good" day, like Christmas or Easter. Invariably these books have been written by authors whose Sunday schools average 1,500 or more, who live in large metropolitan areas, and who run a fleet of buses. In the small Sunday school, I believe that the philosophy should be different. In a small Sunday school where you are still trying to generate a winning attitude, a normally "big" day is a *great* day for a special emphasis. First of all, it is easier to get your people to invite friends to Sunday school on a special day. Also, the ones whom they invite are more likely to come on a day like Easter, Christmas, or Mother's Day.

Second, it will give you an excellent opportunity to introduce your teachers and demonstrate your facilities to a group of people who otherwise might not attend. After all, it is your teachers who will mean the success or failure of your Sunday school. You can do everything in your power to get people to come, but if they are to become regular attenders they will do so because they enjoy their class and can relate to their teacher. Clean, comfortable classrooms are important; lively opening devotions are good; a calling program is a must. But your Sunday school will rise and fall on the strength of your teaching staff. (Teacher training will be discussed in a later chapter.)

Third, a big crowd will generate enthusiasm. Nothing draws a crowd like a crowd. Why? Because wherever you see a crowd, something is happening! Gather 25 people together in a vacant lot in a small town on a Saturday afternoon, and within 30 minutes you'll have 100 people there! How do you get that *first* crowd? That is the advantage of planning your special emphasis for the special day. Your attendance will naturally be up, and with a little extra effort you can set a new record!

We stress every special day that we can think of, and then make up a few of our own. You should have a special day of some kind every month, an extraspecial day every quarter, and a superspecial day twice a year. As long as your special days involve people, they will bring out people. Our two "Super Sundays" are Christmas Sunday and, about six months later, our vacation Bible school program.

Vacation Bible School

We schedule our VBS for the first or second week of summer vacation. At this time our youngsters are still in the habit of going to school, and most vacations and summer recreation programs are not yet under way. We have tried various types of VBS sessions. In a "small" Sunday school, it is usually difficult to get staff members to commit themselves to two weeks of teaching, so we schedule ours for just five days, and run morning and afternoon sessions. We have each child bring a sack lunch, and the VBS supplies the punch at noon. We begin at 9:30 a.m. and run until

11:30 a.m. After a half-hour break for lunch, our afternoon session runs from 12 noon until 2 p.m. This schedule is maintained Monday through Friday. On Saturday we have program practice and then a VBS picnic. Sunday morning during the regular Sunday school hour we have the VBS program, followed by an open house showing handwork, crafts, and our facilities!

We stress remaining for the morning worship service as a family. We of the "small" Sunday schools have a bit of an advantage in our presentations since we can work every pupil into the program, thereby providing each parent with an incentive to come that day. Parents will attend to see their child perform, even if that child is only part of a group song!

Christmas

Our other "Super Sunday" is the Sunday before Christmas. Again, we include every child in our Christmas program. The date for the program is set during our September planning session, so it is known well in advance. This program, too, is held during the regular Sunday school hour, followed by a family worship service.

In our calling program, we attempt to get the entire family to come to Sunday school. If this is not successful, we try for the children and then involve them in activities that will bring their parents out to see them. We always follow a special emphasis in our Sunday school by a special worship service. Don't allow a Sunday school program to rob you of the opportunity of ministering to the parents in a worship service. Most of the parents and youngsters who come on a special day plan on staying for "the whole ball game" anyway. Why not take advantage of this? Going to Sunday school and staying for church are good habits—and we encourage good habits!

Maybe a combined program would work well in your situation. We tried one this year and topped our previous attendance record of 273 by 70. That's right—we had 10 percent of the entire population of our town in our Sunday school on Christmas Sunday!

Our program was designed to use every class from nursery through junior high for a speaking part or song, a teen choir singing familiar carols, a choral choir reading scripture, a portion of the program from some members of the adult and young adult classes, and a message by the pastor. Too many churches pass up the opportunity to "show their wares" to a large crowd. Give them something attractive to remember you by and they will soon come back!

How do you set an attendance record of 343 in a sanctuary that seats 200? We kept all of our program participants in their classrooms until the time came for their presentation, then took them back to their classroom for a treat and the Christmas story after they finished.

For shorter programs, we use one-third of the classes for each program. In this way, every child in Sunday school is in three programs per year—VBS, Christmas, and one other. A shorter program on these days enables you to still have a 30-minute class period, and affords you an excellent opportunity to introduce parents and other guests to their appropriate classes.

On Mother's Day we have a small gift for each mother. A handkerchief, bookmark, sachet, or other small gift, for each mother present, plus several special gifts for some of the following: oldest mother, youngest mother, mother with youngest baby, mother with most progeny present, mother who came the greatest distance to Sunday school, and so forth. One year we used rosebushes for our special awards, and then gave each mother present a packet of flower seeds.

Father's Day emphasis is similar. The small gift can be fishhooks, comb, bookmark, or the like. A month before Father's Day, get baby pictures of as many fathers in your Sunday school as you can. Display these on a poster identified only with numbers. Have any Sunday school member who desires submit an entry guessing the names of the fathers in the pictures. On the big day, identify each of the pictures and give an award to the person getting the most correct.

HONOR-THE-GRADUATE SUNDAY

Have the date for this Sunday correspond with your high school baccalaureate. Alert all of your junior high and high school graduates to wear their traditional graduation gowns on this special day. Reserve pews in the front of the sanctuary for your graduates, and after the congregation is seated for the worship service, and just before the invocation is given, have your pianist or organist play a processional. At this time, have the graduates march in and take their places.

Before the message, have a place in your service for an honor roll call of all your graduates. Have them come forward one at a time to receive an appropriate gift, along with a short recitation by the pastor of some special accomplishment on their part. The message of the morning should be centered about the graduates.

At the conclusion of the service have the congregation hold their places until the recessional is played and the graduates have time to form a receiving line at the rear of the church. In this way your people may congratulate them as they leave the sanctuary. Remember—Sunday school is people, and people count. Use every opportunity to involve people—for people involved will involve other people.

THE GOOD OLD DAYS

Many Sunday school activities are centered around youth, and this is good. But if you need to boost your Adult

Department, the "Good Old Days" will do it. Here is a chance for the "old folks" to have some fun! Several weeks before the "day," announce that you are encouraging people to celebrate the "Good Old Days" at your Sunday school. Encourage them to wear costumes from the "good old days," whether they be maxis, deacons' coats, bonnets, bib overalls, or whatever. Also encourage your people to bring antiques, with a word of explanation on a small card, to display on this special day. Have several tables set up in the front of the sanctuary to display these antiques.

If you can obtain a pump organ for your organist to play for this Sunday, it will make the day an even greater success. Have your pastor speak on "The Old-time Religion," sing songs of yesteryear for the congregational singing. A good number for your choir or singing group would be "Give Me That Old-time Religion." Set lamps about the church, and be sure to "pass the hat"—collection plates are a no-no on the "Good Old Day!" During opening exercises in Sunday school, tell about some of the antiques and mention that others will be identified and discussed during the morning worship service. Tie these two services together as much as possible.

Following your morning worship service have an old-fashioned potluck dinner in your fellowship hall or social center. This day will soon become an annual event by popular demand.

Baby Day

Baby Day can be an effective outreach emphasis for your Sunday school. If you announce the occasion at least four weeks ahead of time, all of your people can be on the lookout for new members to be added to the Cradle Roll on this special Sunday. During the week immediately preceding Baby Day, your Cradle Roll superintendent should contact the parents of each baby on your roll, as well as the parents of prospective members. The function of the Cradle Roll department should be explained to them, and a special invitation to be present for Baby Day should be given. Explain also the nursery facilities that you have available for parents of young babies during Sunday school and church. Later in the same week, be sure that each set of parents previously contacted receives a special invitation in the mail telling them of the exact time and place of the special service.

On the "big day," call all parents and their babies to the front for a special baby gift (comb, brush, powder, lotion, and so forth). Have several appropriate readings or poems; then ask the pastor or superintendent to offer a special prayer in behalf of the babies and their parents. Encourage the parents to attend one of your adult classes, and to remain for worship, reminding them of the nursery facilities and personnel available. Make this a real day of outreach.

Did you ever see a baby come to church or Sunday school alone? When a baby comes, there will be two, three, or even more people with him. Enroll a baby and you are well on the way to enrolling the entire family. The Cradle Roll provides the initial contact, opening the way for a continuing ministry to both the child and his parents. Why not put "baby power" to work for your Sunday school today?

There are a number of other days which may be incorporated into your total program. These will be listed here briefly, with some comments. You may enlarge on these and fit them into your total program, if you so desire.

TEEN DAY

This is a day for your youth group to see how many teens they can have in Sunday school. Plan a special party for the week following to honor all those who attended on this special day.

Bible Day

A twofold emphasis may be used here. Announce several weeks in advance that you want everyone to bring a Bible and also to bring as many different translations as possible. Encourage those who have Bibles that are printed in other languages to bring those, too. Have a special table in the front of the sanctuary to display these, along with a short description of each Bible. Find out who has the oldest Bible present, and display it, giving special recognition to its owner. Encourage your teachers to have a 10-minute Bible drill in their classes, with the students looking up familiar scriptures and reading them.

Children's Day

Urge each youngster to bring a friend to Sunday school on this day. Award a small prize to each child who brings a visitor, and also one to the visitor. Have several short readings about children, and sing children's songs and choruses.

Valentine's Day

For "atmosphere" have each class prepare a large red heart several weeks prior to Valentine's Day. On a piece of white poster board the same size, outline a heart and write the names of the class members willy-nilly all over it. Then cut out the names, making pieces similar to a jigsaw puzzle. During the week before Valentine Sunday, mail each class member his piece and encourage him to bring it to class Sunday, so that it can be pasted in its proper place on the red heart. "Save your class from a broken heart."

Assistant Sunday

A good way to break any rut-forming habits and keep your assistant teachers from feeling that their task is not important is to set apart a day in which they take over. Regardless of your Sunday school size, there always seems to be a shortage of good teachers; but if you do have a more or less complete staff of teachers and assistants, schedule the third Sunday of every month as "Assistant Sunday." Use your assistant secretary and superintendent as well as all of your assistant teachers on this day. It will give them a sense of confidence and valuable experience. At the same time it will give your regulars a rest day and your classes a change of pace. It will be beneficial in every way to everyone. It also makes it much easier for the assistant to step in when illness keeps your "regular" at home.

Memorial Day—Independence Day

For each of these special days, sing patriotic songs in your opening. It is also a good idea to repeat the pledge of allegiance to your country's flag, the pledge to the Christian flag, and the pledge to the Bible. Honor any servicemen present in your service by having them stand while you tell their rank, branch of service, and where they are stationed. Make a poster several weeks in advance and display it in the foyer on this day. The poster should have a picture of each serviceman who is connected with your home church, along with his address. Encourage your folk to write or send a cheery card. Have your young people meet for a party, at which time they can bake and package boxes of cookies, candy, and other goodies and mail them to your men in the service.

Thanksgiving

Stress thankfulness on this special day. Sing songs of thanksgiving in your opening exercises. Take a special offering on this day for a special missionary project. Encourage children to share their abundance in this way. Have your teachers stress thankfulness in their classes on this Sunday, making the children aware of the many things that we have for which we should give thanks.

Church Birthday

Do a bit of research, if necessary, and find out the date that your church was founded. This might be the date the first service was held, the date the cornerstone was laid, the first service in your present building, or the date the church was organized, whichever would be the most meaningful for your people. Announce that each person present in Sunday school on that day will receive a piece of birthday cake. Bake, or have baked, a large sheet cake with appropriate decorations for the age of your church—some candles, lettering, frosting, and so forth. If you have an unretired building debt, or are starting a building fund, construct a small wooden replica of your present facility (or of the proposed building) with an opening in the roof that an offering will pass through. Have your pianist play an appropriate song while the people march up to place their offering in the "church" and receive their piece of birthday cake.

Promotion

Promotion Sunday can be an important day in your Sunday school if you will plan for it in advance. Your approach will, of course, vary with the age level that you are dealing with at that particular time. For the nursery through all of your primary classes, crepe-paper capes and hats with crepe-paper tassels will really make a hit. For junior through teen classes, merely reading the name of the youngster and presenting the certificate is sufficient.

In addition, to help the younger children make the adjustment from their present class to their new one, try the following idea: At the beginning of the promotion, have your nursery teacher and his or her class gather in the front of the sanctuary. The Cradle Roll superintendent should then read the names of those children on the roll who are two or three years of age, and have them take their place in the front with the nursery class. The next class (fours, preschool, or whatever you have) is then called to the front of the sanctuary on the other side, along with their teacher. The nursery teacher then reads the names of the children that she is promoting. They receive their certificates and take their places with their new class. The nursery teacher then takes her class and goes to her classroom. The next class (first grade or whatever) comes to the front with their teacher, and the preschool class teacher reads the names of those that she is promoting. They receive their certificates and move to their classroom. The whole process is then repeated until you will eventually have only your adults left in the sanctuary, and they may then go to their classroom as well. You will find that this process will get your promoted youngsters into their proper class with less fuss and tears than any other, and yet it affords each pupil that important bit of recognition. It also will serve as an icebreaker for the new student moving into class, and will help to integrate your new class members with the old.

For this day, as for all special days, send special invitations to the involved parents by letter, phone calls, or personal contact. Never pass up an opportunity to recognize a child for some special achievement, and when you give that recognition, be sure that you have alerted his parents to attend.

Are special day programs worth the effort put into them? They are if your planning is right. Here are some helpful hints: Plan a worthwhile program. On Father's Day, for example, a series of recitations about Father will have sentimental value, but how about also including a short panel discussion on "How to Lead Family Worship"?

Promote effectively. Word-of-mouth invitations by children to their unsaved parents are not enough. If the program is worth having, it is worth advertising through all media possible.

Keep the program uncomplicated. A simple program allows for more thorough preparation and minimizes last-minute frenzy and haste.

Remember that Bible study is the main goal of your school. Do not cut down or do away with the regular class session because of the program. Having encouraged people to come, give them a sample of a regular Sunday school class session.

Expect visitors and prepare for them. Have a welcoming committee stationed at the door whose only task is to make visitors feel welcome and show them where to go.

Follow up new contacts immediately. This is the only sure way to keep them coming after the special day has passed.

Special day programs can either become a monumental headache, repeated several times annually, or they can be an effective form of Sunday school outreach. Start today to make the special days in your school really count.

One last word on recognition. In a small Sunday school where the chances are good that you know every student there, watch your local paper for notices that some of your Sunday school scholars have received recognition in scouting, school, 4-H, and so forth. Mention this in your class or in the church service the following Sunday and have the individual stand and give him applause. (A bit of hand-clapping once in a while in your Sunday school will help to liven up the atmosphere and take away some of the stiffness and starchiness that might be present.)

Your Sunday school should *not* be a miniature church service. Loosen up—make it lively and interesting—*have fun!* People want to be where the action is!

Chapter 3

Contests and Attendance Campaigns

In addition to the emphasis on special days, contests are also good for helping Sunday school growth. They may be as short as a 4-week promotion, or as long as 10 weeks. They should probably not be shorter than 4 weeks, because it takes a while to "get rolling"; and anything longer than 10 Sundays usually gets old and boring for those involved.

Listed below are a few hints to help make any enlargement campaign a success:

Get the church building and grounds in good repair. Evaluate and improve the music program. Organize ushers. Watch the time schedule—don't waste a minute. Keep sanctuary and classroom lighting and decoration in good repair. Make arrangements for the extra finance necessary to run the campaign. Outreach advertising is essential to supplement person-to-person contact. Publicity should include individual mailings. Every possible name and address should be gleaned from old Sunday school records—children of parents, parents of children, neighbors, and friends. Get names from Welcome Wagon and schools.

Use every possible source of names and phone numbers. *A church will not grow by working and reworking the same old names. But* never drop a name. These *must* be passed on to the next pastor and Sunday school superintendent and the next one and the next one. Keep the name of every individual who ever comes or shows any interest in the church. Unless he dies, moves out of town, or becomes an active member of another church, keep in touch with him periodically. Every department of the church must assist in follow-up.

Every class should be organized for both outreach and follow-up. Make names available so that everyone can make contacts by phone, mail, or visit, and plan a way to recognize those individuals who *do* make contacts. This is vital.

Sing familiar songs during any outreach campaign. Sunday school classes should be decorated to go with the theme, and seating arrangements should be changed to indicate a special event.

Contests with Other Sunday Schools

If there is another Sunday school of your denomination in your area, challenge them to an attendance contest. If they are of somewhat equal average attendance, your contest can be on a straight numerical gain. If you challenge a much larger or much smaller Sunday school, you will have to work on a percentage basis. Set up your contest so that the concluding Sunday will fall on one of your special days. This type of contest is best run on a six- or eight-Sunday basis.

On your Sunday school record board, which should be prominently displayed in the sanctuary or foyer where it may be seen by all, put your Sunday school name and also the name of the one you are challenging. Keep a running attendance total, cumulative from Sunday to Sunday.

There are a number of ways that you can keep in contact with each other and generate enthusiasm at the same time. One very simple method is, of course, by merely writing letters back and forth, which can then be read in the other Sunday school on the following Sunday morning. A much better method is to use a cassette recorder, so that you can mail tapes back and forth. These can then be played in opening exercises or in individual classes. These tapes should contain a record of the attendance for that particular Sunday, and some special message or challenge to the other. You can make the tape right during the Sunday school hour. It might include a recording of your Sunday school singing a favorite chorus, a special number by some of your Sunday school members, a short word from the pastor or superintendent.

If your situation lends itself, there should be a bit of joshing or bragging about the victory that you are going to win over the other Sunday school—anything that will generate a bit of enthusiasm. Tapes may be constructed at home, using sound effects from records to emphasize your message.

The last Sunday of the contest, you should arrange with the other Sunday school to have a phone call put through at the conclusion of Sunday school, so that you may have the final results of the contest immediately. The telephone company can hook this up to the speaking system, or to special speakers, so that all can hear. This will give you immediate results and tell you who the contest winner is. In a contest of this sort, nobody ever loses, because any gain that either of the Sunday schools makes in attendance makes it a winner! Let your imagination work for you in this type of contest. One Sunday school that challenged us here in Buffalo served pieces of cooked buffalo meat to everyone who attended on a specific Sunday!

We like to stress having entire families in Sunday school and worship, so this promotion has worked well for us. It should run for a four-Sunday month. Begin your promotion by designating a specific month as Family Month. Set aside particular Sundays to honor various members of the family. Make the first Sunday "Baby Day" or "Nursery Day" and honor all of the families that are present who have babies on the Cradle Roll (or who are willing for their baby to be enrolled) and/or in the nursery class. Contact these families the week prior to Baby Day and give them a special invitation to attend. Recognize publicly all the little ones who are present on Baby Day and have a small gift for each one. Emphasize the importance of your Cradle Roll and have the superintendent of the Sunday school present a small appreciation gift to the Cradle Roll superintendent.

Designate the second Sunday as "Children's Day." Have a short program about children in the home, and have a small treat for each child present. Again, stress to your congregation the importance of children in your Sunday school and church. Also recognize publicly the teachers of these children and the work that they do each week in preparing for their classes on Sunday. (Give your Sunday school teachers recognition whenever possible—it will encourage them to work even harder.)

The third Sunday should be "Parents' Day." Here's a chance to express gratitude to the moms and dads who faithfully *bring* their children to Sunday school week after week. Have several poems or readings which stress the importance of a Christian home. Point out the advantages inherent in entire families worshiping together. Commend parents for their part in bringing their families to the church for worship and study.

The last Sunday should be "Family Foto Sunday." Announce on each Sunday of Family Month that on this final Sunday you will take a free photograph of each complete family present on "Family Foto Sunday." A complete family unit should include all those members of the family who are living at home and who are physically able to attend Sunday school. The pictures may be taken in a variety of ways. If your budget is in good shape, you can hire a photographer to take the pictures as the families arrive. For smaller budgets, you might have a good amateur photographer in the crowd who has a Polaroid camera. You could purchase the packs if he would take the pictures. (In our case, the superintendent used his Instamatic, flash cubes, and colored film. The film was mailed to the processor on Monday, was back on Thursday, and the pictures were displayed on a poster on Sunday.) Leave the pictures up for two weeks, so that everyone can see them, and then present the picture and the negative to the family. This sounds simple, and it is, but *it works!*

It is not so much the magnitude of the promotion gimmick as it is the interest that is shown in individuals that builds a Sunday school. Encourage your people to be a happy, enthusiastic group and to sell Sunday school wherever they go. Talk Sunday school, preach Sunday school, think Sunday school!

Race Cars

Obtain a piece of ¼-inch pegboard at your local lumberyard. The board should be wide enough so that each class can have a strip two inches wide with a one-inch space between each. The total width of the board will be governed by the number of classes. Paint the board, and either number or name the two-inch strips across the bottom from the youngest to the eldest class. At the top of each lane, write the average attendance of that class for the previous three months. Mount this pegboard on the wall where it can be seen by all.

Have each class bring a toy car, fire engine, pickup, or what have you, not more than two inches in length, to represent their class. Using long pieces of ribbon (the crinkled, stretchy, paper kind used at Christmas works well), attach the front of each car to one end of the ribbon and then thread the ribbon through the top and bottom holes and fasten to the backs of the cars. This will form a continuous ribbon. Position all the cars at the bottom of their respective lanes. Assign a value to each hole of the pegboard from the bottom to the top, so that the top hole reads a little more than the maximum expected gain of any one class.

A car may progress each Sunday by the number in class *above* the average attendance indicated. Adjust each car before Sunday school begins each week, and watch the enthusiasm mount as the "race" progresses. The winning class should be given recognition the week following the "race," and perhaps the Sunday school should treat them to ice cream or a hamburger, whatever would fit that age-group. Tickets for the latter can usually be purchased at a local drive-in, then presented to the class during opening exercises.

THERMOMETER

If you are striving to break a current record, this idea might help create interest. Using a frame of lumber and a front of cardboard or wallboard, construct a large thermometer at least 12 inches wide and 6 to 8 feet tall. Number the thermometer from the bottom to the top, starting with your recent average attendance at the bottom and going up to your new attendance goal. Divide the spaces in between these two points equally and number every other one or so to show continuity and yet readability. Make two wooden tracks out of quarter round, from bottom to top, in which a block of wood 1 x 6 x 6 inches can slide. Attach a strong string or twine to the top of the block and thread it over a pulley or smooth notch at the top of the thermometer. Fasten a wide red ribbon on the bottom of the block, with the excess ribbon rolled up behind the thermometer. (It should feed out at your lowest number.) This arrangement should allow you to pull the string from behind, thus raising the "temperature" in your thermometer. At the top of the thermometer mount a large balloon, and on the top edge of the block fasten a large pin. When you reach your goal, the sharp pin will "pop" the balloon. This works well for about a six-weeks promotion.

Top 20 Day

This idea can be adjusted to your average class size. If most of your classes average fewer than 10, you could have "Top 10 Day," and so forth. The idea is to encourage classes over a four- or five-week period to make contacts for Sunday school.

On your Sunday school record board, create a category which reads, *"Contacts."* Prepare a 3 x 5 card, like the accompanying sample, marked off for the four or five Sundays involved. Have one of these cards filled out by each teacher or class secretary each Sunday and picked up by your Sunday school secretary, along with your regular class report. The teacher should ask each member of the class how many invitations to Sunday school were given the past week and record the total class contacts on the card. The total of contacts should then be posted and attention called to it in both Sunday school and church. Make the last week "Contact Week" and see how many contacts the entire Sunday school can make. The object is for each class to "Top 20" in attendance on the final day, illustrating to your people what contacts can do for your Sunday school.

CLASS __________________		TEACHER __________		
		CONTACTS		
March 1	March 8	March 15	March 22	March 29

A number of incentives can be offered for contacts made. For the children, a 15-minute plane ride over your city or town might be arranged. For the teen or adult making the most contacts, dinner for two at a local restaurant could be an incentive reward. You may, if you are trying to break an old record, announce that the pastor will break the old record over the superintendent's head. (Prepare an old 78-rpm record and paint the current record attendance number on it. When this attendance figure is exceeded, break the record. If the superintendent's head can't take it, use a hammer on the record instead.)

TOTEM POLE

A simple device to encourage a class to break its average attendance is the totem pole. Using a base board 2″ x 12″ x 12″, attach a pipe collar so that a threaded, ½-inch, galvanized pipe about three to four feet long (depending on the number of classes you have) can be screwed into the collar. Make, from roughened blocks of wood about four inches on a side, small totem faces in many colors and expressions.

You will need one for each class, and they should have a
⅝-inch hole drilled through them so that when they are
slipped onto the ½-inch pipe, they form a totem pole.

The first Sunday, all the "totems" should be on the
pole, and each should be identified for the class it represents.
Thereafter, for four or more Sundays, just the "totems" of
the classes which exceed their average attendance are left
on the pole.

The success of this type of subdued attendance drive
will depend largely on the emphasis and recognition that you
give to your totem pole, and to the classes which are reach-
ing their goal.

The Ten Commandments

Probably one of the most successful attendance campaigns which we have ever conducted was "The Ten Commandments." Available from Wright Industries, 139 Loretta
Drive, Dayton, Ohio 45415, for less than $1.00 per pupil, it
consists essentially of giving each person in Sunday school
an attractive key chain or bracelet and awarding charms,
each containing one of the Ten Commandments, each time
they attend.

We set our campaign for a normally slack 11-Sunday
period in early spring. The first Sunday, every person
present is given a key chain or bracelet and the campaign is
introduced. For the next 10 Sundays, each person present is
given a small charm imprinted with one of the Ten Commandments, to attach to his chain or bracelet. Those who
are absent on a particular Sunday can pick up the commandment they miss by bringing a visitor on a subsequent Sunday during the campaign. The key chain or bracelet should
be given to anyone coming for the first time, no matter what
Sunday that is, and charms missed can then be earned by
bringing visitors.

Additional meaning can be given to the campaign and the commandments by having your Sunday school classes take turns presenting a short playlet or reading during the opening devotional period which illustrates the commandment for that day.

For example, our nursery class had the commandment, "Honour thy father and mother." They repeated the commandment in unison, and then each set of parents was called to the front and presented with a small gift by their toddler. Our young adult class had "Thou shalt not commit adultery." A husband and wife of that group, along with the pastor, went through a 10-minute wedding ceremony, repeating and renewing their vows. This proved meaningful to adults and children alike.

HOMECOMING

Set up this four-Sunday promotion so that the final Sunday falls on the weekend of your local high school's homecoming. Announce several Sundays ahead of time the details of your promotion, so that all may be alerted, prepared, and enthused!

Divide the youth and children's division of your Sunday school into four general categories: preschool, primary, junior, and teen. Before your promotion begins, have the teachers of all of your preschool classes, including the nursery class, get together and choose a boy and a girl from *each* preschool class to represent the preschool department. Elect one girl and one boy as queen and king, and allow the other children chosen to be attendants. Honor these children on the first Sunday with a gift appropriate to their age level. Alert the parents of these children before the presentation Sunday, so that they may be present. If possible, take a Polaroid picture of the "royalty" and place on a poster for all to see. At the same time, have all classes from second grade up vote for a teen king and queen to be crowned the last Sunday of the promotion.

On the second Sunday, honor the primary youngsters in the same way. That is, choose two representatives from each primary class. Designate one boy as king and a girl as queen, allowing the others to be attendants. Notify parents and award small, appropriate gifts. Take pictures and post. Again, cast ballots for teen king and queen.

On the third Sunday, use the same procedure with your junior classes. On this Sunday conduct the final balloting for teen king and queen.

On the fourth Sunday, honor the teen king and queen who have been chosen by ballot, as well as the royalty from all of the preceding Sundays. Separate, and also group, pictures may be taken. Present your teen king and queen with gift certificates from a local clothing store. All of the ceremonies described can take place during your 15-minute opening devotional period and need not interfere with regular class time. Decorations can be fashioned after those at a high school homecoming with pennants, streamers, pompons, and so forth.

Chapter 4

Other Ideas

Balloon Sunday

For an extraspecial, one-Sunday promotional idea, try a "Balloon Sunday." We recently used this promotion, and found it to be a huge success.

Before you set up your "Balloon Sunday," decide on an attendance goal for your Sunday school. Order more than enough balloons for that record number. These may be purchased from any supply house that deals in Sunday school materials. Also, see a local compressed-air company and acquire a tank of helium with a special attachment to fill balloons. You can purchase a tank of helium that will fill 250 balloons for about $30.00. Plan on one cubic foot per balloon, since helium is purchased by the cubic foot.

Four weeks before "Balloon Sunday," announce that every person present on "Balloon Sunday" will launch his own balloon with his name tag attached. Also announce that everyone whose tag is returned will receive a gift. The one whose tag is returned from the farthest distance will receive a $10.00 bill, while the second farthest will receive a $5.00 bill.

We recently used this promotion, using regular mailing tags about 2 x 4 inches in size. The following message can be typed on the back of each tag:

My name is _______________________.

I attend the _______________________

Sunday school in _______________________.
If you will mail this tag back to me
to the address on the other side by

_______________________, you will

receive a gift and so will I.

We set a cutoff date of six weeks hence. This is necessary so that prizes can be awarded before interest wanes.

The second Sunday, five or six helium-filled balloons were brought into the opening and allowed to float up to the ceiling with long strings attached. "Balloon Sunday" was again stressed. The third Sunday, just prior to "Balloon Sunday," every person present was given a tag and told to place his name on it and leave it in his classroom in readiness for the next Sunday.

On "Balloon Sunday," a group of about eight people met early in a large room and began filling 250 balloons with helium, and tying them with 12-inch strings. (*Caution:* This must be done on "Balloon Sunday" morning, since helium diffuses rapidly through balloons. If you fill them on Saturday evening, they will all be flat by Sunday morning.)

Opening exercises consisted of just an opening chorus or two and prayer. Then all were instructed to go to their classrooms, pick up their tags, and proceed to the balloon room. Extra tags were provided for those who were not present the previous Sunday. The adult classes received their balloons first, then assisted the younger children in tying their tags onto the balloons. Soon all of the people in Sunday school had filed out to the church parking lot, holding tightly to their balloons. When all had their balloons in hand (a few escaped early), we all counted down, 5—4—3—2—1—GO! and over 200 balloons began their rapid ascent.

During the next six weeks a total of nine tags were returned—two from as far as Iowa, almost 700 miles away! Letters were written to the individuals who returned the tags, and a Christian plaque was mailed to each one.

Dial-a-Ride

Looking for a different approach? Try the ad below in your local paper once a week for a month, several times a year, and see the results that you obtain. Line up people in your Sunday school from different areas of town, so that they can stop by and pick up those needing rides on their way. Usually these will be children; but if you'll work at it, their parents will soon be bringing them, and staying themselves!

A number of other one-Sunday promotions will be listed here. Most of these are presented as a basic structure—the "meat" will come from the adaptation to your situation.

Fall Roundup

In the fall, sponsor a "Back-to-School Day," or call it the "Fall Roundup." It's a good way to get those summer vacationers back into the habit of attending Sunday school again. Here in Wyoming we have everyone who cares to do so wear western clothes for our "Fall Roundup." We stress bringing in the strays and the dogies, and getting our Sunday school brand on them. A small pin can be given to each with your church name as a "brand."

Attendance Pins

While we're on the subject of pins, you should look into one of the attendance pin plans that are advertised by Christian supply houses. Most award a small pin when the person becomes a member of the Sunday school, another pin for three months of perfect attendance, one at six months, and a permanent pin for nine months of perfect attendance. Year bars for each year of perfect attendance are awarded after that. These will hold a great appeal for many people, and are well worth the expense. You will need an attendance secretary to keep records of attendance. One of your adult ladies who is willing to invest the time will do a good job at this. Be flexible in your rules for "perfect attendance." In case of difficulty, it is much better to bend and award the pin than to lose a Sunday school member.

Host and Hostess

Your Sunday school should elect from year to year a *host and hostess*. These should be people who meet others well, and who are friendly and outgoing. The host should remain at the door until classes have taken up, to assist latecomers in finding a place to sit and, later, in finding their classes. To assist the host, you should post on the bulletin board in your foyer a list of every Sunday school class, the age-group for that class, the teacher and assistant teacher, and the location of that class. Nothing will turn a visitor away faster than the rush to "pass to classes," leaving them trampled, muddled, and confused. *Hint:* Try allowing your teachers to go to their classrooms first; then dismiss the rest of the Sunday school. You will be surprised how this will cut down on the noise and confusion, and it will allow your teacher to be in the classroom when the pupils arrive. Of course, if the opening activities are held in the individual classrooms or departments, this particular problem will be taken care of.

Your hostess should sit at a small table in the foyer. She should be familiar with each member of the Sunday school, so that she can recognize visitors when they arrive. She should have a form on which the visitor lists his name and address, and whom he is a guest of, if this be the case. A lapel badge may also be placed on the visitor's dress or coat, giving the teacher and other class members instant notice that a visitor is in their midst. These badges can be cards or ribbons and are available from supply houses. The cards should be made available to superintendent, teacher, and/or pastor, so that each visitor can be welcomed by name at the appropriate time, telling whether he is from in town or out, and of whom he is a guest. The little time spent in mentioning a visitor by name is well worth it if thereby that visitor later becomes a member.

The visitor's card is then relayed to those responsible for follow-up. If the visitor returns for a second Sunday, he should be asked if he would like to be enrolled as a member of the Sunday school. If he answers in the affirmative, then he should be called to the front, and the initial membership pin presented to him. (We also change the enrollment figure on the Sunday school register at the same time, so that he can see that he actually caused our enrollment to change.)

Vacationers' Map

Another way to welcome visitors in the summer months, if you are in an area that attracts tourists, is this: Obtain a large map of the United States (at least three feet by four feet). Also purchase several small packages of flag stickers. Display the map at the front of the sanctuary mounted on the wall, or on a piece of lightweight insulation board, so that it can be moved with ease. Every time you recognize an out-of-town visitor, place a flag sticker over the name of his hometown on the map, and see how many states are represented by the time the summer is over. If your own people have guests in their homes, this will encourage them to bring them to Sunday school, so that their hometown, too, can be represented.

Another interesting effect can be obtained by having your own people bring back a church bulletin from each church they attend while they are on vacation. These bulletins, too, can be displayed at the front of the sanctuary. They will serve as an interest point as well as an encouragement to your own people to attend church and Sunday school while they are on vacation. Tell them to be alert to new ideas that they may encounter on their trip, and invite them to share these ideas with the class on their return.

Above all, be a friendly Sunday school. A few years ago my family was vacationing right here in the state of Wyoming, though several hundred miles from home. We had spotted an independent church not far from our motel and decided to worship there, hoping to perhaps glean some new insight and ideas to take home to our own situation. We arrived about 10 minutes before the scheduled starting time, in a driving rainstorm. We hurried into the church foyer, only to be greeted by stares from about six people.

Leaving my family in the foyer to endure the stares, I proceeded toward an open door marked, "Pastor's Study."

I saw a gentleman in the study, so knocked briefly on the door casing to attract his attention. I asked him if there was an adult Sunday school class available. He replied, as he sailed by me toward the stairs, "I don't know, but the pastor's around here someplace." I returned to the foyer, and after waiting several minutes with no one as yet even speaking to us, we returned to the car and drove down the street to another Sunday school, where we were received warmly.

Now it is true that we were in town for only that one Sunday, and have not had occasion to be back there on a Sunday since. But if we ever do, can you guess where we will attend Sunday school? And suppose that we had just moved into town and that had been our first Sunday looking for a church home? How many visitors who are looking for a church home do you drive away? We can invite and promote, advertise and encourage all we want; but if we're not friendly at the front door, all will be lost.

Elective Courses

Another good idea to add some spice to your Sunday school is to offer an elective course. This can be taught during the regular lesson hour, to supplement, not necessarily replace, your other offerings. We try to offer at least one elective per year, and would rather offer two. We are presently offering a 12-week elective on how to build a Christian home. This will be followed by a course in teaching methods for prospective Sunday school teachers. Adults will come to your Sunday school only if they *want* to come. Parents might tell their children to go, and for a while they might. But adults will come only if they feel that they are receiving something worthwhile for the time they are investing. Make your Sunday school something that all age-groups will *want* to attend, and watch it grow!

Lost Purses

What is your first reaction when you find a purse or billfold? You look to see what's inside! Here is a suggestion you may want to try which capitalizes on the natural curiosity of those living in your church neighborhood.

Several weeks prior to your special day, ask your people to bring any and all of the old purses and billfolds that they may have around. Also have them contact their neighbors and friends so that as many of these as possible can be collected. Have the purses brought as soon as possible, so you can get an idea of how many you have and/or how many more you will need.

The week prior to your special day, mimeograph an invitation to your Sunday school and church, including the following verse, and insert it in the purses:

> *This purse has no money,*
> *But please do not fret.*
> *The message inside it*
> *Is far better yet.*

The next step is to have the youth of your church meet on Friday evening to distribute these purses after dark. Leave them on doorsteps, curbs, or lawns where they will be obvious to the residents the next morning. If possible, choose houses in the church neighborhood where you are certain the people do not attend church elsewhere.

Redeem Your Coupon

Sometime during the week before a special Sunday, mail to all those on your roll a coupon that has been mimeographed or printed. On this coupon you will want to put an invitation, the name and address of your Sunday school and church, the hour of services, and any other pertinent information. If a person brings a visitor on that day, his coupon can be redeemed. There are two suggested ways that can be used to designate what the gift may be. (Both would have to be kept secret.) One is to have the coupon double thickness and have the gift sealed inside. The other is to have it written on the coupon with lemon juice, which is legible only when held close to the heat of a candle.

Anyone for a Puzzle?

Have an enlargement made from a snapshot of your church; then cut it into approximately one-inch squares. The size will depend on the number of squares needed to accompany your special day invitation to all active, inactive, and prospective Sunday school members. (An 8 x 10 photo will yield 80 pieces, for example.) Also have a replica drawn on white paper. Number the backs of the cutout squares to match numbered squares on the replica. Along with your special day invitation, mail a puzzle square for each member of the family, asking all to come and help put the puzzle together. Keep a record of each square as mailed out. Place the replica in the lobby, and as each person enters on your special day, have him put his square in its place.

IDEAS FOR RALLY DAYS

Many Sunday schools label at least one special Sunday a year as Rally Day—a day to rally in all the folk you can. Listed here are several ideas to help promote your Rally Day.

Rally Day Breakfast

A Rally Day breakfast is a wonderful way to get the new Sunday school year off to a good start, and the formula for a successful breakfast is really quite simple. First, of course, you need enthusiasm. In addition to posters and invitations, make sure that the children of your school know about the coming event. You can depend on them to be up earlier than the appointed hour, prodding reluctant parents and friends out of bed. Next, find a good "eggs 'n' bacon" cook. The menu is irrelevant, but if it tastes good, you'll find "Sunday school enthusiasm" growing with every bite. Third, but most important, you need a pastor and people who care. Don't be surprised to see some strange faces at your breakfast, and by all means, get to know the newcomers. That personal touch will be the thing that brings them back again.

Senior Citizens

Encourage your senior citizens to have *all* members of their family attend with them on Rally Day. Then have a photographer take their family picture. Post it on the bulletin board and present it to them at a later date.

Treasure Chest

Either locate an old trunk-type chest or have one built and enclose a gift; then lock it up. Display this chest at Sunday school, and on Rally Day give each person a key for every visitor he brings. Have the ones with keys come forward and try each key in the lock. The person with the key that fits receives the gift. (Be sure the right key is given to someone.)

Each One Bring One

This pretty well explains itself. Other titles you can give it are "Twin Sunday" or "Bring Your Double." To make it more of a challenge, the week prior to Rally Day give everyone half of an item, with instructions that he will receive the other half if he brings a visitor on Rally Day. An example would be to give the shell of a ball-point pen. If the person comes and brings a visitor on Rally Day, give him the refill part. Another idea that could be used with this would be to have ribbons with "Rally Day" printed on them. If a person brings a visitor or visitors, attach a colored seal for each one brought. See whose ribbon has the most seals.

Do You Have Your Reservation In?

Select several calling teams with two on a team, and have them visit the homes of your absentees and prospective members the week prior to Rally Day. While they are still in the home, and if they receive a promise to attend, have them call back to the church or parsonage and make a reservation for Rally Day. This may even be carried so far as to reserve a pew or portions of a pew with the names of those who have placed a reservation. Be sure to keep the telephone lines as open as possible during this time, and keep your conversations as concise as possible, so as to enable all the calls to come through.

Roll Call

Secure a roll of paper (shelf paper works fine) on which to write all of the names of those who attend your Sunday school. Hang it where all can see it on Rally Day morning. You will probably need a ladder to reach the names at the top. The pastor and/or superintendent will call the names, marking them present or absent. Introduce the following chorus the Sunday preceding Rally Day (sung to the tune of "When the Roll Is Called Up Yonder, I'll Be There"):

> *Let's get up on Sunday morning and get out to*
> *Sunday school,*
> *Let the weather be so stormy or so fair.*

Then today and every Sunday this will always be
the rule,
When the roll is called next Sunday, I'll be here.

Chorus
When the roll is called next Sunday,
When the roll is called next Sunday,
When the roll is called next Sunday,
When the roll is called next Sunday, I'll be here. *

If your school is so large that listing all the names is impractical, try this: Call the names of the heads of the households represented in your congregation. Have them stand and tell how many they brought with them.

Coded Message

To generate enthusiasm in a class or department, particularly at the primary—junior level, try sending a coded message to each pupil during one particular week of the month. Tell him that in order to decipher the code he must attend Sunday school the following Sunday to receive a code key. You can code the message by scrambling letters, or by using various symbols for the letters.

Have the deciphered message a special one, so that students will look forward to it each month. Use a different code each time, of course. Your message might announce a party, a meeting for Cokes and hot dogs, or the location of a special prize. Some of the greatest times your class will ever have are the times when you meet or take them to an inexpensive hamburger place for a hamburger and a soft drink.

*Courtesy of the *Wesleyan Advocate*.

Chapter 5

Teacher Training

So far in this book we have been largely concerned with getting people to *come* to Sunday school. Equally, if not more important, however, is what we do with those pupils once we get them there. Your Sunday school will be no more effective for the kingdom of God and His Church than the effectiveness of your teachers. That is, if you are to have a quality Sunday school, you must have quality leadership.

"Yes, I know," you probably are replying, "but where can we get effective teachers and officers for our Sunday schools? In the church where I worship there simply are not enough outstanding persons who qualify."

For this question, as for so many other questions which arise in various areas of the church's ministry, we find guidance toward an answer in the teaching and practices of Christ himself.

For this particular problem, He set a notable example when He chose the 12 men into whose hands He was soon to entrust the full responsibility of leading on in His redemptive mission among men. After a long night of earnest prayer before the Father, He picked a group of very ordinary men from common walks of life. None of them possessed religious or political influence. None of them had experience in teaching or preaching. None of them were men of the schools. They were not particularly conspicuous for their insights or ideals.

But something of what He had in mind for them is evident in His words to Simon and Andrew as Mark recorded them. He said, "Come ye after me, and I will make you to become fishers of men" (1:17). Note the words "to become." He did not promise that instantaneously or in some miraculous manner He would give them power and authority over other persons. He told them that under His training they were to give themselves to *becoming*. With His teaching and guidance they could become the kind of leaders He needed. Under His tutelage, they could develop the necessary attitudes and skills. Just as they had learned the sea and the fish through years of diligent application, so now with similar application they must learn about the gospel, implement it into their own lives, and learn the best ways to present it.

This concept of leadership was much in the mind of the Apostle Paul. He wrote to Timothy, a younger pastor in Ephesus: "The things which you have heard from me in the presence of many witnesses, these entrust to faithful men, who will be able to teach others also" (2 Tim. 2:2, NASB).* This New Testament concept has important implications for the solution of our present-day local church leadership problems. It suggests that if we are going to have adequate leaders we must start with the persons we have. We can't wait until the prepared and promising come to us.

*From the *New American Standard Bible,* copyright © The Lockman Foundation, 1960, 1962, 1963, 1968, 1971.

Those more or less common people who have opened their hearts to the Lord and attend our churches may have potential no more conspicuous, either to themselves or to us, than those apostles had when Jesus called them from their fishing, their tax collecting, and other such occupations.

Perhaps we need to pray for seeing eyes, that we may recognize obscure potential and then set about to motivate, recruit, and train available persons. Most people who refuse to teach a Sunday school class do so because they are not sure just what is expected of them. They need self-confidence in order to undertake a teaching ministry. It is the job of the Sunday school to train its own teachers. You wouldn't expect the public schools to put an untrained teacher in your child's classroom, nor would you stand for it if they did. How much more important that we have trained teachers in the Sunday school classroom teaching children eternal values!

We tried a rather simple training method and doubled our teaching staff in six months. First, we explained to the entire Sunday school for several Sundays in opening activities that we needed to train teachers for our expected increase. We stressed the importance of a Sunday school teacher to the kingdom of God, to the local church, and to themselves. Teaching a Sunday school class is a God-given opportunity to present His Word to others and must *not* be taken lightly. Many of the children that a teacher faces on Sunday morning will not hear Christ mentioned except in cursing, until the following Sunday morning. Many children receive their only spiritual training for the entire week from their Sunday school teacher.

In presenting this need and challenge, we stressed the fact that we would run the teacher training class twice, for three months each time. We wanted half of our regular teachers to take the class during the first three months, along with enough assistants to relieve the second half when the time came. After the initial training period, those trained were to relieve those teaching, so that they could then take the course. We then went to each Sunday school class, teen through adult, and presented the accompanying Survey Sheet. We asked our people to prayerfully fill it out and turn it in at the end of the class period. When the final results were tabulated, we had more than enough people who volunteered to teach as assistants for the necessary period.

We set up our teacher training class for the same time period as our regular Sunday school classes. At the conclusion of the period, those who had completed the course took over the Sunday school classes, and those who had been teaching enrolled in the course. If you have a public school teacher in your Sunday school, he is an excellent choice for teaching these courses, since they largely incorporate those methods used in public schools. A methods course will give your teachers the self-confidence that they need and will train a ready staff of assistant teachers as well. Some such courses should be conducted annually, to accommodate new people in the Sunday school and keep a prepared group of teachers at hand.

The importance of a trained teaching staff cannot be stressed too strongly. Unless we provide a quality teaching program which interests and affects those people who attend, it will be better if outsiders do not come. If they come once and are disappointed in what they find, it will be much harder to get them back than it was to get them to come in the first place. And even worse, this will result in negative publicity in the community, making it hard to interest others.

Less than quality teaching also shortchanges our own church people who attend regularly through loyalty. Too often the periods set aside for classes are boring periods of idle talk or lecturing about religion with nothing really happening. With proper planning and with prepared teachers, however, those times can be among the most interesting, inspiring, faith-building, and redeeming experiences in the church's ministry.

The Lord expects us to go out and bring people in, all kinds of people. But when they do come, we must have things going which will interest them, influence them, win them, and hold them.

Sunday School Workers Survey

I am interested in seeing our Sunday school grow. God being my Helper, I am willing to do my share of the work by serving in any of the positions that I have checked below, for the coming church year,

or (dates) _________________ to _________________.

_____ Sunday School Superintendent
_____ Assistant Superintendent
_____ Sunday School Secretary
_____ Sunday School Treasurer
_____ Teacher of Children
_____ Teacher of Teens
_____ Teacher of Adults
_____ Assistant Teacher of Children
_____ Assistant Teacher of Teens
_____ Assistant Teacher of Adults
_____ Sunday School Host
_____ Sunday School Hostess
_____ Cradle Roll Superintendent
_____ Home Department Superintendent
_____ Sunday School Usher
_____ VBS Teacher
_____ VBS Helper
_____ Sunday School Bus Driver
_____ Sunday School Bus Driver Assistant
_____ Sunday School Pianist
_____ Member of Program Committee (plan Christmas program, and other programs)

Signed: _________________________________

Chapter 6

Tips for the Superintendent

In this final chapter, I would like to share, with God's help, some of the things that He has helped me to glean in my work as a Sunday school superintendent.

First of all, that superintendent is fortunate whose pastor has Sunday school on his heart—who realizes that the Sunday school is in no way in competition with the church program. The two should be mutually supportive.

Secondly, the superintendent needs an enthusiastic, dedicated staff of workers. They may not be highly trained professionals (though good teachers constantly seek to improve their skills), but they do need to be loyal and willing to be used of God.

Lastly, the superintendent needs an eager group of pupils. These are the "salesmen" who let everyone know that they attend the *number one* Sunday school in the community! It may or may not be the largest Sunday school in town, but it's the best! It is known as the place where things happen!

* * *

Here are 20 random tips for the Sunday school superintendent:

1. *Be Enthusiastic.* You set the pace for the Sunday school. If you become discouraged, you will soon pass this spirit on to staff and pupils.

2. *Expect Much.* Your staff will respond to your expectations. Expect little and you'll receive little. Expect your teachers to be on hand every Sunday, to begin lesson preparation early in the week, to arrive early for each session, to attend workers' meetings, and so forth.

3. *Love Your Staff.* These are your workers, giving of themselves unstintingly. Show your appreciation. The New Testament Church was famous because of their Christian love one for another.

4. *Compliment Achievement.* If you are going to admonish against failure, you must compliment achievement. A verbal "pat on the back" from a sincere superintendent will work wonders in the life of a hardworking staff member, even if the achievement is minimal.

5. *Pray for Your Sunday School.* Make Sunday school the number one item on your prayer list. Pray for yourself, your staff, your pastor, and your pupils.

6. *Live Sunday School.* Let it infiltrate every area of your life. Always be on the lookout for new ideas, new methods, and a chance to invite someone to Sunday school.

7. *Accept Suggestions.* You'll be criticized. The only way to avoid making a mistake is to do nothing—and that's a mistake. Let your staff know that you are willing to accept suggestions for the improvement of the Sunday school.

8. *Start on Time.* If your people assume you will start late, they will arrive late. Don't wait on anyone. Arrive early

58

yourself, get organized, and at the *exact* starting time, *start*. It may take some months, but eventually your people will begin to arrive on time.

9. *Plan Ahead.* Plan your special days, your staff meetings, your campaigns. You should have a yearly planning meeting to outline the basic program for the year.

10. *Make Staff Meetings Worthwhile.* Don't just have a meeting because it seems the thing to do. If you can't make your staff meeting one hour or less in length and useful to your staff, don't have one!

11. *Stress Teaching.* Compliment your teachers publicly. Stress the rewards of teaching. Expect to have good teachers. Sponsor teacher training programs.

12. *Set Goals.* Concentrate on your objective and don't worry about the negatives. If you anticipate all the reasons why something won't work, you will never venture to do anything. As someone has said: Be an engineer, not a brakeman.

13. *Compete Against Last Year.* Have last year's attendance on your register. Strive continually to be ahead of last year. God is interested in numbers in your Sunday school, for every number is a soul. You are here to see that every pupil is given the glorious gospel.

14. *Define Objectives.* This goes much beyond mere attendance figures. There is no limit to what you can achieve. The only real limitations are the ones you impose upon yourself. Define the objective. What is it you want to achieve? Most people don't really know what they want to accomplish. Defining the goal or objective is always the starting point of achievement.

15. *Make the most of available time.* Time is precious in Sunday school. In many instances time is wasted because students straggle in late, because too much time is given to meaningless activities, and because interruptions are al-

lowed. Run a "tight ship," for Sunday school time is short enough at best.

16. *Involve People.* Involve as many as possible in Sunday-school-related positions. Every job is important because it makes for personal involvement. It may be handing out bulletins, teaching a class, holding babies in the nursery, or leading singing for a department. This is an argument for breaking down the school into smaller classes—fewer spectators, more workers. Use more personnel and promote individuality.

17. *Strive for Bible Study.* A Bible carried to Sunday school may not necessarily be a Bible studied previously, but under the guidance of a wise teacher it will be put to use in class. In time, the thrill of Bible discovery may result in home Bible study as well. The Bible is the Sourcebook in all Sunday school teaching, and each pupil should be urged to bring his Bible to class.

18. *Plan a Dedication Service for Your Staff.* Many Sunday schools now schedule an annual dedication service for teachers and officers. This may be held at the beginning of the Sunday school year as a part of the Sunday morning church service. The pastor asks all teachers and officers to come forward for the ceremony. The purpose of this service is threefold. It gives public recognition to Sunday school workers; it impresses them (as well as the congregation) with the magnitude of this work; and it unites the church and Sunday school in a closer way.

19. *Schedule an Annual Appreciation Banquet.* Sunday school workers give countless hours without remuneration —often in unrecognized tasks. Once a year do something really nice for them. Challenge the church people who are not involved to help pay the bill. Awards for special achievements, the naming of the "Teacher of the Year," and so forth, could be features of this annual event.

20. *Strive for Church Attendance.* How unfortunate to see an exodus of people immediately following class sessions! Youngsters (and older ones) who go home after Sunday school fail to learn the art of worship or to reap its benefits. Never forget that the Sunday school is part of the church, not a separate organization. Worship goes hand in hand with Bible study as a goal worth striving for.